3A

FOUR CORNERS

Second Edition Workbook

JACK C. RICHARDS & DAVID BOHLKE

CAMBRIDGE
UNIVERSITY PRESS

CAMBRIDGE
UNIVERSITY PRESS

University Printing House, Cambridge CB2 8BS, United Kingdom

One Liberty Plaza, 20th Floor, New York, NY 10006, USA

477 Williamstown Road, Port Melbourne, VIC 3207, Australia

314–321, 3rd Floor, Plot 3, Splendor Forum, Jasola District Centre, New Delhi – 110025, India

103 Penang Road, #05–06/07, Visioncrest Commercial, Singapore 238467

Cambridge University Press is part of the University of Cambridge.

It furthers the University's mission by disseminating knowledge in the pursuit of education, learning and research at the highest international levels of excellence.

www.cambridge.org
Information on this title: www.cambridge.org/fourcorners

First published 2012
Second edition 2019

20 19 18 17 16 15 14 13 12 11 10 9 8 7 6 5 4

Printed in Italy by Rotolito S.p.A.

A catalogue record for this publication is available from the British Library

ISBN 978-1-108-55859-4 Student's Book with Online Self-Study 3
ISBN 978-1-108-55980-5 Student's Book with Online Self-Study 3A
ISBN 978-1-108-55982-9 Student's Book with Online Self-Study 3B
ISBN 978-1-108-61762-8 Student's Book with Online Self-Study and Online Workbook 3
ISBN 978-1-108-65810-2 Student's Book with Online Self-Study and Online Workbook 3A
ISBN 978-1-108-67667-0 Student's Book with Online Self-Study and Online Workbook 3B
ISBN 978-1-108-45935-8 Workbook 3
ISBN 978-1-108-46076-7 Workbook 3A
ISBN 978-1-108-45936-5 Workbook 3B
ISBN 978-1-108-55995-9 Teacher's Edition with Complete Assessment Program 3
ISBN 978-1-108-55999-7 Full Contact with Online Self-Study 3
ISBN 978-1-108-56013-9 Full Contact with Online Self-Study 3A
ISBN 978-1-108-56292-8 Full Contact with Online Self-Study 3B
ISBN 978-1-108-45940-2 Presentation Plus Level 3

Additional resources for this publication at www.cambridge.org/fourcorners

Contents

Credits

The authors and publishers acknowledge the following sources of copyright material and are grateful for the permissions granted. While every effort has been made, it has not always been possible to identify the sources of all the material used, or to trace all copyright holders. If any omissions are brought to our notice, we will be happy to include the appropriate acknowledgements on reprinting and in the next update to the digital edition, as applicable.

Photography
The following photographs are sourced from Getty Images:
U2: Juice Images/Cultura; **U3:** Eva Mueller/The Image Bank; Steve Gorton/Dorling Kindersley; Ghislain & Marie David De Lossy/The Image Bank; Siri Stafford; Steven Errico/Digitalvision; Alija/Istock; Stockbyte; Evening Standard/Stringer; Fotosearch; Ryan Miller/Contributor; **U4:** Tyler Stableford/Aurora Outdoor Collection; **U5:** Winhorse; Hisham Ibrahim; Laura Ciapponi; Paul Souders; Altrendo Travel; Oliver Strewe; Achim Thomae; Image Makers; Doug Armand; Ascent/Pks Media Inc.; **U6:** Ty Milford; Kerkez/Istock Jossdim; Walterbilotta; Jeffrey Coolidge.

The following photographs are sourced from other libraries:
U1: Gulfimages/Alamy Stock Photo; Klaus Tiedge/Blend Images/Media Bakery; Michele Falzone/Alamy Stock Photo; **U3:** Zee/Alamy Stock Photo; Rtimages/Alamy Stock Photo; Deco/Alamy Stock Photo; Doublephoto Studio/Shutterstock; Karkas/Shutterstock; **U4:** Chris Ryan/ Ojo Images/Media Bakery; Mario Lopes/Dreamstime; Front cover by Hero Images; Eva-Katalin/E+.

Illustration
QBS Learning.

Front Cover by Sergio Mendoza Hochmann/Moment; Betsie Van der Meer/DigitalVision; andresr/E+. Back Cover by Monty Rakusen/Cultura.

Education

A I'm taking six classes.

1 Look at the pictures. Write the correct school subjects.

1 chemistry

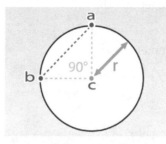

2 g_____

3 w_____

g_____

4 m_____

5 h_____

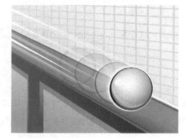

6 p_____

7 b_____

8 a_____

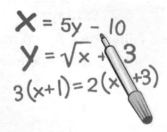

9 a_____

2 Complete the sentences with the correct school subjects from Exercise 1.

1 Sandra's favorite classes are science classes: _____chemistry_____,
_____, and _____ .

2 John has two math classes: _____ and _____ .

3 Leo's favorite classes are in the arts: _____ and _____ .

4 Mi-hee is taking two social studies classes: _____
and _____ .

3 Check (✓) the correct sentences. Rewrite the incorrect sentences with the correct forms of the verbs. Use the simple present or the present continuous.

1 ☐ Dina reads her email right now.
   <u>Dina is reading her email right now.</u>

2 ☐ Tim is knowing a lot about biology.
   _____

3 ☐ Mateo and Alicia are taking a dance class together.
   _____

4 ☐ I'm wanting to study in Australia in the summer.
   _____

5 ☐ What is the word "engineer" meaning?
   _____

6 ☐ Do you go to class right now?
   _____

7 ☐ They don't remember the answers for the history test.
   _____

8 ☐ This homework isn't seeming difficult.
   _____

4 Look at the schedule. Complete the sentences with the correct forms of *work*. Use the simple present or the present continuous.

Officemart Summer Schedule			
Name	**Fridays**	**Saturdays**	**Sundays**
Marcia	2:00 p.m. – 8:00 p.m.	9:00 a.m. – 3:00 p.m.	✗
Leo	10:00 a.m. – 5:00 p.m.	9:00 a.m. – 5:00 p.m.	12:00 p.m. – 4:00 p.m.
Paul	✗	2:00 p.m. – 7:30 p.m.	✗

1 Marcia and Leo _____ work _____ on Fridays and Saturdays.

2 It's Sunday, and Marcia and Paul _____ .

3 It's 11:00 a.m. on Friday. Leo _____ .

4 It's 3:30 p.m. on Saturday. Leo and Paul _____ right now.

5 Leo _____ on Sunday afternoons.

6 Paul _____ on Fridays.

7 It's 6:00 p.m. on Friday. Leo _____ right now.

8 Marcia and Leo _____ on Saturday evenings.

2

5 Complete the text messages with the correct forms of the verbs in parentheses.
Use the simple present or the present continuous.

J.Monk78	Hi, Shelly. What ____are you doing____ (do) right now?
	₁
SLP1980	Hey, Jin-sung. I _____ (write) to you! 🙂
	₂
J.Monk78	Very funny! _____ you _____ (study) for the chemistry test?
	₃ ₃
SLP1980	Yes, I am. Linda and I _____ (read) the teacher's notes online.
	₄
J.Monk78	I _____ (not / understand) those notes at all.
	₅
SLP1980	_____ you _____ (want) some help?
	₆ ₆
J.Monk78	Yes, please!

Emmie	Hey, Kate. What classes _____ you _____ (have) on Fridays?
	₇ ₇
KateM	I _____ (have) algebra in the mornings and geometry in the afternoons.
	₈
Emmie	What time _____ (be) your geometry class?
	₉
KateM	At 2:00. Wait . . . my sister _____ (call) me . . .
	₁₀
KateM	OK. I'm back. My sister _____ (shop) right now. Let's go to the mall.
	₁₁
Emmie	OK, but I _____ (work) right now. How about at 11:30?
	₁₂
KateM	Great! Let's meet in front of Los Zapatos Shoe Store.

6 Answer the questions with your own information. Write complete sentences.

Example: ___I'm taking English, physics, and music.___

1 What classes are you taking? _____

2 When do you study? _____

3 How often do you have English classes? _____

4 Where do you usually do your homework? _____

5 What school subjects do you like? _____

6 What school subjects do you hate? _____

7 What are you doing right now? _____

8 Where are you sitting? _____

B You're not allowed to . . .

1 Complete the chart with the sentences from the box.

> ✓ You can't use your cell phone in the office.
> You have to come to work by 9:00.
> You must always wear a suit to work.
>
> You need to have lunch at that time.
> You're not permitted to eat in your office.
> You're not allowed to write emails to friends.

Prohibition	Obligation
You can't use your cell phone in the office.	

2 Complete the conversation with the correct sentences from the box in Exercise 1.

Ms. Jones Welcome to Akron Accounting. This is your new office. Do you have any questions?

Mr. Okada Yes. Can I make personal phone calls at work?

Ms. Jones No, I'm sorry. _You can't use your cell phone in the office._
1
You can make personal calls at lunch.

Mr. Okada OK. What time is lunch?

Ms. Jones It's from 1:00 to 2:00.

_____ .
2

Mr. Okada Can I have lunch at my desk?

Ms. Jones No, I'm sorry. _____ .
3
You can have lunch in our café, or you can go out to eat. There are a lot of good restaurants on Pine Street.

Mr. Okada OK. Thanks. Is there anything else I need to know?

Ms. Jones Yes. _____ .
4
We try to dress for business here.

Mr. Okada No problem.

C My behavior

1 Look at the pictures. Complete the puzzle with the feelings and emotions you see.
What's the mystery word?

1

2

3

¹T	H	I	R	S	T	Y

4

5

6

2 Complete the sentences with the correct words from the box.

hungry	jealous	scared	✓ thirsty	upset

1 Miguel wants some water. He's _____thirsty_____ .

2 Carla didn't eat lunch today, and now she's very _____ .

3 John's team didn't win their soccer game. He's extremely _____
about it.

4 Paula is an actress. Mariana wants to be an actress, but right now she's a waitress.
She's _____ of Paula.

5 When Peggy came home last night, her front door was open. She was
_____ and called the police.

5

3 Complete the conversation with *if* and the correct words from the box.

I have a job interview	I'm prepared	there's a website
I'm nervous	she's home	✓ you're nervous

Carmen Hey, Danielle. What do you do

_____ if you're nervous _____ ?
1

Danielle _____ about
2

something, I try not to think about it.

Carmen Well, I have a job interview tomorrow, and
I have to think about it!

Danielle Hmm . . . _____ ,
3

I usually prepare before I go. It really helps.

Carmen How do you prepare?

Danielle _____ , I read about the place online.
4

Carmen That's a good idea.

Danielle Yes. I also practice the interview with my sister _____ .
5

Carmen I can try that with my brother. What about during the interview?

Danielle _____ , I usually don't get nervous. Good luck!
6

4 Combine the sentences into one. Use *when*. Write it in two ways.

1 Emma has a test. → She studies a lot.

When Emma has a test, she studies a lot.

Emma studies a lot when she has a test.

2 I get bad news. → I get upset.

_____

_____

3 Jordan gets up early in the morning. → He is sleepy.

_____

_____

4 My sister is busy. → She doesn't call me.

_____

_____

5 Lorena and Jessie have a soccer game. → They get nervous.

_____

_____

5 Write sentences in the zero conditional. Use the words in the chart.

Condition	Main clause	If / When
1 Tonya's sister / go to a party	Tonya / always / get jealous	when
2 Greg / be lonely	he / often / call a friend	when
3 I / get scared	I / always / call my brother	if
4 Kyle and Rick / be busy	they / sometimes / not eat	if
5 Leticia / get angry	she / usually / not say anything	when
6 I / be late for work	I / usually / say I'm sorry	if

1 ___When Tonya's sister goes to a party, Tonya always gets jealous.___

2 _____

3 _____

4 _____

5 _____

6 _____

6 Write questions with the words in parentheses. Use *What* and the zero conditional.

1 (Charlie / do / if / be sleepy)   *What does Charlie do if he's sleepy?*

2 (you / do / when / get upset)   _____

3 (Frank and Julie / do / if / get angry)   _____

4 (you / do / if / be hungry)   _____

5 (you and your friends / do / when / be thirsty) _____

6 (Annette / do / when / feel nervous)   _____

7 Answer the questions with your own information. Write complete sentences with the zero conditional.

Example: ___When I'm nervous about a test, I study really hard.___

1 What do you do when you're nervous about a test? _____

2 What do you do if you're sleepy in class?   _____

3 How do you feel when you're too busy?   _____

4 What do you do when you're lonely?   _____

5 What do you drink if you're thirsty?   _____

6 What do you say when you're angry with a friend? _____

D Education controversy

1 Read the article. Answer the questions.

1 Who works for a magazine? _____

2 Who works for an engineer? _____

Work-Study Programs in High School

Many high schools in the United States have work-study programs. In their last year of high school, some students have a job for part of the day as one of their "classes." Some of these students make money and some don't, but all of them learn important things about having a job and being a good worker. Many people think that when students learn outside of the classroom in a real job, they prepare for life after high school. Work-study programs can really help students get a job or get into college.

There are many types of work-study programs. Most of the students work in offices, but not all of them do. Some students fix cars, and others work outside with environmental engineers. Big businesses, like computer companies and banks, often work with high schools to create work-study opportunities for students as well.

Raul Gomez usually goes to school from 9:00 a.m. to 4:00 p.m., but this year he works for a magazine from 7:00 a.m. to 11:00 a.m. He says, "I learn important things in my work-study program. I must be at work on time. And if I miss a day, they don't pay me!" At work, he reads stories and fixes spelling and grammar mistakes. He says, "At work, I use what I learn in my English class. And now I think that someday, I might want to write for a magazine or a newspaper."

Raul Gomez at his work-study job

Annie Miller works for an engineer in her work-study program. They design and help make bridges, roads, and buildings. She says, "It's great! I love learning math in school, but at work, I use algebra and geometry in the real world!"

Not all high schools offer work-study programs. But most of the schools that have them think they are a big success.

2 Read the text again. Then write T (true), F (false), or NI (no information).

1 Work-study programs started in the United States. ___NI___

2 Some students get money in work-study programs. _____

3 Work-study programs rarely help students start their careers or further their education. _____

4 Raul works at his job in the morning. _____

5 Annie likes science classes. _____

6 Not many of the work-study programs are a success. _____

Personal stories

A What were you doing?

1 Put the letters in the correct order to make adverbs. Complete the sentences.

(y u o u t r n l f t a n e)

1 I was having a great
   day on Tuesday. Then,
   _____unfortunately_____, I
   left my bag at a restaurant.

(l l i c y u k)

2 _____,
   someone found it.

(l y f e t o a n u t r)

3 And _____,
   my cell phone was in
   the bag.

(l s y r u i n s g i p r)

4 _____,
   the person who found it called
   my home phone.

(a z n i g a y m l)

5 _____, the person was David, a boy I went to
   school with when I was six! We made plans to meet at a café.

(y e s t a r g l n)

6 _____,
   David looked the same! We
   ate lunch and talked a lot.

(s n u e y d d l)

7 Then David got a phone
   call, and he left the café
   _____.

(s a y l d)

8 _____,
   I never saw him again.

2 **What were they doing when the lights went out? Write sentences with the
past continuous forms of the verbs.**

1 (Mi-na / read / a book)

   Mi-na was reading a book.

2 (Martin / wash / the dishes)

3 (Brad and Kate / watch / TV)

4 (I / talk / to Tom / on the phone)

5 (Laura / play / video games)

6 (Mr. and Mrs. Jones / eat / dinner)

3 **Complete the sentences with *when* and the words in parentheses.
Use the simple past forms of the verbs.**

1 (their friends / arrive)

Jane and Paul were making dinner on Friday _when their friends arrived_ .

2 (his brother / call)

Martin was driving to the store _____ .

3 (the electricity / go off)

What were you doing yesterday _____ ?

4 (Jill / send me / a text message)

_____, I was talking to Tom on my cell phone.

5 (the ambulance / come)

What were they doing _____ ?

6 (the storm / begin)

_____, I was walking home from work.

4 Complete the conversation with the correct forms of the simple past or the past continuous of the verbs in parentheses.

Rick Hi, Lisa. What _____were_____ you _____doing_____ (do)
$_1$

when the electricity _____went_____ (go) off?
$_2$

Lisa Unfortunately, I _____ (work)
$_3$

on the computer! I couldn't finish my work. What

_____ you _____ (do)?
$_4$ $_4$

Rick Oh, I _____ (sleep) when
$_5$

everything _____ (go) dark.
$_6$

I didn't even know what happened.

Lisa Really? It was only 7:30 p.m.

Rick Well, I _____ (take) a nap in the living room. I think I slept
$_7$

for a long time. When I _____ (wake) up, it was really dark.
$_8$

So I just went to bed. While everyone else _____ (have) problems,
$_9$

I _____ (sleep)!
$_{10}$

5 Complete the story with the verbs in the box. Use the past continuous or the simple past.

✓cook	go	make	stand	turn
fall	hear	see	try	

Terry and Wendy _____were cooking_____ in the kitchen when the electricity suddenly
$_1$

_____ off. Unfortunately, while Terry _____ to find
$_2$ $_3$

a light, he _____ down. He _____ a loud noise when he fell.
$_4$ $_5$

When Wendy _____ the noise, she _____ by the window.
$_6$ $_7$

While she _____ around, she _____ something move outside
$_8$ $_9$

the window. What was it?

6 Answer the questions with your own information. Write complete sentences.

Example: _I took biology, history of China, and English last year._

1 What classes did you take last year? _____

2 What were you saying the last time you spoke? _____

3 Where did you eat breakfast today? _____

4 What did you do last night? _____

5 What were you doing at 6:00 a.m. today? _____

6 What were you doing when class started? _____

B Guess what!

1 Write A (announcing news) or C (closing a conversation).

1 Listen, I've got to run. _____C_____

2 You'll never guess what happened! _____

3 Sorry, I have to go. _____

4 Hey, I need to get going. _____

5 Guess what! _____

6 Did you hear what happened? _____

2 Complete the conversations with the sentences from Exercise 1. Sometimes more than one answer is possible. Use each sentence once.

A. **Jim** Hello, Pat. <u>Did you hear what</u>
                        ₁
            <u>happened?</u>

   Pat No, I didn't.

   Jim There was an accident on Main Street.

   Pat That's terrible!

   Jim Yes, it is. Fortunately, everyone is OK.

            _____ .
                  ₂

   Pat OK. Bye.

a car accident

B. **Annie** Hey, Tonya! _____ !
                                      ₁

   Tonya What?

   Annie Martin got a promotion, and he's moving to Canada.

   Tonya That's great.

   Annie I know. _____ . I have a meeting
                              ₂
             in a few minutes.

   Tonya No problem. Call me later!

C. **Beth** Hi, Dan. _____ !
                                  ₁

   Dan What?

   Beth Our soccer team won the competition.

   Dan That's fantastic! _____ . I have
                                      ₂
           class now. But congratulations!

   Beth That's OK. Thanks. See you tomorrow.

C I was really frightened!

1 Put the letters in the correct order to make verbs that describe reactions.

1 i e t e c x _____excite_____   5 g e t h f i r n _____

2 d u s s g i t _____   6 a u e s m _____

3 s o u n f c e _____   7 e c n l a g h l e _____

4 i t t n r s e e _____   8 s m a e s a r b r _____

2 Complete the conversations with the correct forms of the verbs in Exercise 1.
Use the simple present.

1 **Nancy** Hey, Karl. Did you do the homework for math class?

 Karl No, I didn't. Geometry _____confuses_____ me. I don't understand it.

2 **Po** Jill. Try this sushi.

 Jill No, thanks. Fish _____ me! I hate it!

3 **Larry** My brother talks too loudly. He really _____ me when
he's with my friends.

 David It's not so bad. He's very friendly.

4 **Tom** What _____ you, Seth?

 Seth Horror movies! I get really scared when I watch them.

5 **Ted** Do you like animated movies?

 Lea Yes, they usually _____ me. I think they're funny.

6 **Ahmet** Chemistry _____ me, but I think physics is boring.

 Andrea Really? I think physics is interesting.

7 **Miho** What do you want to do this weekend? Anything exciting?

 Karen Well, the idea of going to Chicago for the weekend _____ me!

8 **Eva** You're pretty good at sports, Tim. What kind of sport _____ you?

 Tim Golf, I guess. It's a lot more difficult than it seems.

3 Complete the sentences with the present participles (*-ing*) or past participles (*-ed*) of the verbs in parentheses.

1 Amusement parks are _____*exciting*_____ (excite).

2 Can you help me? This physics problem is _____ (confuse).

3 I want a new job because my work is too easy. I don't feel _____ (challenge).

4 I don't think your problem is _____ (embarrass). A lot of people talk fast when they're nervous.

5 I'm _____ (frighten) by our neighbor's dog! It's big and extremely loud.

6 I'm not _____ (interest) in math, but I love science.

7 I don't think video games are _____ (amuse), but many teenagers like them.

8 My brother is _____ (disgust) by reality shows, but I'd like to be on one!

4 Circle the correct words to complete the conversation.

Paul   Hi, Wendy. Have you ever read *Life of Pi*? You know . . . that story about a boy who is on the ocean in a boat with a tiger.

Wendy Yes, I have. I liked it, but I thought some parts with the tiger were **disgusted** / **(disgusting.)**
1

Paul   Really? I thought it was **frightened** / **frightening**, but I was **excited** / **exciting** when I read it.
2   3

Wendy Well, yes, it was **excited** / **exciting**. But after a while, I think Pi was probably **bored** / **boring** on that boat. He was on it for 227 days!
4   5

Paul   Oh, I don't think so. I bet life on that boat wasn't **bored** / **boring** at all! I loved how he became friends with the tiger. That was really **interested** / **interesting**.
6   7

Wendy Yeah. That part was **amused** / **amusing**, I guess, but it didn't seem like real life.
8

Paul   Maybe not, but I think the story shows that sometimes life is **challenged** / **challenging**.
9

Wendy Yeah, you're right. And I guess the end was **surprised** / **surprising**.
10

Paul   Um, well . . . now I'm **embarrassed** / **embarrassing**. To be honest, I didn't finish the book!
11

14

5 Read Ron's online survey. Then complete the sentences about Ron's opinions.

We want to hear from you!

1 What kind of music are you interested in?

☑ rock   ☐ jazz   ☐ blues   ☑ hip-hop

2 What do you think of concerts?

☑ exciting   ☐ boring   ☑ amusing

3 Who are you embarrassed by?

☐ your parents   ☑ your brothers and sisters   ☐ your friends

4 What do think about technology?

☑ confusing   ☑ challenging   ☐ easy

5 What kinds of foods do you think are disgusting?

☑ fish   ☐ meat   ☐ fruits   ☑ vegetables

1 Ron is _____ interested _____ in _____ rock and hip-hop music _____ .

2 He thinks _____ concerts _____ are _____ .

3 He is _____ by _____ .

4 He thinks _____ is _____ .

5 He thinks _____ are _____ .

6 Write sentences about your opinions with a participial adjective from the box.

Example: _____ I think horror movies are amusing. _____ *or* _____ I'm frightened by horror movies. _____

amused / amusing	disgusted / disgusting	frightened / frightening
bored / boring	embarrassed / embarrassing	interested / interesting
challenged / challenging	excited / exciting	surprised / surprising
confused / confusing		

1 horror movies _____

2 history classes _____

3 the news _____

4 reading books _____

5 reality shows _____

6 math

How embarrassing!

1 **Read the email. Then check (✓) the correct adjectives.**

1 The hotel is _____ .

☐ interesting   ☐ dirty   ☐ embarrassing

2 The Japanese street names are _____ .

☐ amusing   ☐ challenging   ☐ disgusting

3 Angela did two things that were _____ .

☐ traditional   ☐ interesting   ☐ embarrassing

Hi George,

I'm having an amazing time in Japan! I'm in Kyoto visiting a lot of interesting places. I'm staying in a *ryokan*. It's a traditional Japanese hotel. It's really interesting. The hotel is part of a man and woman's home. Their names are Mr. and Mrs. Ito. I have breakfast by myself at the *ryokan*, and I eat lunch in the city, but I have dinner with the family in their part of the house. Their daughter brings me tea in the evening before I go to bed! This makes me feel like a very important person!

I'm learning a lot about life in Japan, but I'm also doing some embarrassing things by mistake! In the *ryokan*, you take off your shoes before you go in the house so that the floor doesn't get dirty. You leave your shoes outside the door. On my first day, I took off my shoes, but I did it in my bedroom. I walked through the house first, and I got the floor dirty. How embarrassing! I hope Mr. and Mrs. Ito weren't disgusted with me. But they are nice and very friendly, and now I remember to take off my shoes before I come in the house.

I was also embarrassed while I was traveling around the city yesterday. I don't speak Japanese, but I speak Spanish. When I asked for directions, no one understood me! I was pronouncing the street names like Spanish words. They're very difficult to say! But it's easy to get around in Kyoto. The buses and trains are extremely modern and clean. Tomorrow I'm going to an art museum. I'm going to practice pronouncing the museum and street names in Japanese tonight!

It's really fun here. I don't want to go back home!

Your friend,

Angela

---

2 **Read the text again. Then answer the questions. Write complete sentences.**

1 Where is Angela staying in Kyoto? _____

2 Who gives Angela tea? _____

3 What two embarrassing things did Angela do? _____

4 What is Angela's opinion of the buses and trains? _____

5 What is Angela doing tomorrow? _____

Style and fashion

A Fashion trends

1 Look at the pictures. Complete the puzzle with fashion words.

Across

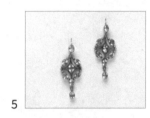

4

5

7

8

Down

1

2

3

6

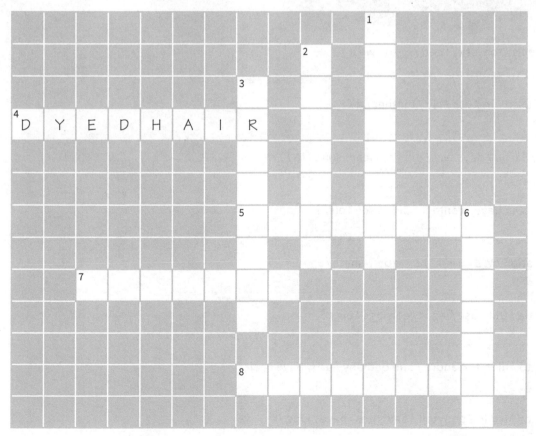

2 **Cross out the fashion word that doesn't belong in each list.**

1 **Clothing**	~~a bracelet~~	a leather jacket	a uniform
2 **Hairstyles**	a ponytail	dyed hair	sandals
3 **Jewelry**	earrings	a bracelet	glasses
4 **Eyewear**	contact lenses	earrings	glasses
5 **Shoes**	sandals	a uniform	high heels

3 **Put the words in the correct order to make sentences.**

1   high heels / to work / used / I / to / wear / .

   I used to wear high heels to work.
   _____

2   wear / used / to / wig / My / mother / a / .

   _____

3   every / Jason / day / use / didn't / wear / suits / to / .

   _____

4   to / lenses / have / contact / Did / use / you / ?

   _____

5   on vacation / We / used / buy / to / T-shirts / .

   _____

6   to / Katia / Did / use / wear / earrings / big / ?

   _____

7   dyed / to / didn't / Sandra / and Bethany / use / have / hair / .

   _____

8   used / a / My / to / ponytail / daughter / have / long / .

   _____

18

4 Circle the correct words to complete each conversation.

1 **A** Did you _____ to have dyed hair?

   B No, I _____ , but I do now.

   a use, did   **b** use, didn't   c used, did   d used, didn't

2 **A** Did Leo _____ to wear a bracelet?

   B Yes, he _____ ! But now he doesn't wear any jewelry.

   a used, did   b used, didn't   c use, did   d use, didn't

3 **A** Where _____ Kelly and Margie use to shop?

   B They _____ to shop at the mall.

   a didn't, use   b didn't, used   c did, use   d did, used

4 **A** What kinds of clothes did Jake _____ to wear?

   B He _____ to wear T-shirts and baggy jeans.

   a use, use   b used, use   c use, used   d used, used

5 **A** Did you _____ to wear glasses?

   B Yes. I didn't _____ to wear contact lenses.

   a use, use   b used, use   c use, used   d used, used

5 Look at Emma's information. Then write sentences with the words in parentheses.
Use *used to* or *didn't use to*.

What did you use to wear?

	1970s	1980s	1990s	2000s
baggy jeans	✓	✗	✗	✓
tight jeans	✗	✓	✓	✓
bright T-shirts	✓	✓	✗	✗
high heels	✗	✗	✓	✓
big earrings	✓	✓	✓	✗

1 (bright T-shirts / the 1970s)   Emma used to wear bright T-shirts in the 1970s.

2 (high heels / the 1970s)   She didn't _____

3 (baggy jeans / the 1980s)   _____

4 (tight jeans / the 1980s)   _____

5 (big earrings / the 1990s)   _____

6 (big earrings / the 2000s)   _____

B Does this come in . . . ?

1 Write the conversation in the correct order.

Can I help you?	Oh, thanks! Um, do you have this in brown?
✓ Excuse me.	They're here, behind you.
No, I'm sorry. It only comes in black.	Yes. Where can I find the leather jackets?

Renaldo _Excuse me._

Clerk _____

Renaldo _____

Clerk _____

Renaldo _____

Clerk _____

2 Write a conversation for each picture with the words in the box and your own ideas.
Use the conversation in Exercise 1 as a model.

Can I get this in . . . ?	Does this come in . . . ?
Could you tell me where the . . . are?	Where are the . . . ?

1 **Debbie** Excuse me.

   Clerk _____ ?

   Debbie Yes. _____ ?

   Clerk _____ .

   Debbie Oh, thanks! _____ in red?

   Clerk No, I'm sorry. _____ .

2 **Ichiro** _____ .

   Clerk _____ ?

   Ichiro Yes. _____ ?

   Clerk _____ .

   Ichiro Oh, thanks! _____ in blue?

   Clerk Yes. _____ .

C The latest look

1 **Read about the types of clothes. Then write the fashion word that matches each type.**

1 clothes that people like right now but might not like next year t r e n d y

2 clothes that are the style that people want or like ___ ___ ___ ___ ___ ___ ___ ___ ___ ___

3 clothes that used to be what people liked ___ ___ ___ – ___ ___ ___ ___ ___ ___ ___ ___ ___

4 new clothes that look like old styles (in a good way) ___ ___ ___ ___ ___

5 clothes that look expensive and exciting (in a good way) ___ ___ ___ ___ ___ ___ ___ ___ ___

6 usually cheap clothes of poor quality or bad style ___ ___ ___ ___ ___

7 clothes that look very strange ___ ___ ___ ___ ___

8 clothes that attract a lot of attention because they're bright ___ ___ ___ ___ ___ ___

2 **Look at the pictures. Complete the sentences with your own opinions. Use words from the box. Not all the words will be used.**

fashionable	glamorous	retro	trendy
flashy	old-fashioned	tacky	weird

Example: ___Her dress is fashionable.___ *or* ___Her dress is flashy.___

1 Her dress is _____ .

2 Her shoes are _____ .

3 Her sunglasses are _____ .

4 His shirt is _____ .

5 His pants are _____ .

6 His hat is _____ .

Rewrite the sentences. Replace *that* with *which* or *who*.

1 I don't like clothes that are trendy.
   I don't like clothes which are trendy.
   _____

2 Tonya is the kind of person that buys things for other people.
   _____

3 I like the kind of store that has a lot of sales.
   _____

4 Is Jason someone that follows fashion trends?
   _____

5 We prefer salesclerks that give us their opinions.
   _____

6 Carla prefers shoes that are not high heels.
   _____

7 Is there a store in the mall that sells sunglasses?
   _____

8 Greg and Roberto are people that always wear retro clothes.
   _____

4

Complete the conversation with *which* or *who*.

Emily Mom, what is a fashion designer?

Mom It's a person _____*who*_____ makes new
                              1
          clothing styles.

Emily And what is a tailor shop?

Mom It's a store _____ has tailors.
                         2

Emily OK . . . but what's a tailor?

Mom Well, a tailor is a person _____
                                      3
          makes or fixes clothes.

Emily Really? OK. And what does a stylist do?

Mom That's a person _____ helps actors look good.
                            4

Emily Thanks, Mom!

Mom Why are you asking me all these questions?

Emily I found this magazine _____ is about fashion. I'm taking a quiz in it.
                                    5

Mom You mean, *I'm* taking a quiz in it!

5 Read the question. Then complete the response with *who*, *that*, or *which* and the correct forms of the verbs and other words in parentheses.

1 A Who is Ms. Young?

   B She is the chemistry teacher <u>who wears</u>
<u>flashy clothes</u> . (wear / flashy clothes)

2 A Does Marvin buy all types of clothes?

   B No, he doesn't. He usually buys clothes

     _____ .

     (be / fashionable)

3 A What kind of malls do you like?

   B I like malls _____ .
(have / a lot of stores with trendy clothes)

4 A Who is Jennifer X?

   B She's a singer _____ .
(wear / weird clothes at her concerts)

5 A Who is Jacques?

   B He's that famous designer _____ .
(make / retro clothing)

6 A What is *Viv*?

   B It's a website _____ .
(sell / old-fashioned jewelry)

6 Complete the sentences with your own information.

Example: <u>Black is a color that I wear a lot.</u>

1 _____ is a color that I wear a lot.

2 _____ is a person who has a style that I really like.

3 _____ is a magazine or website that people read
for information about fashion.

4 _____ is a clothing style that is trendy right now.

5 _____ is a place that sells clothes that I like
to wear.

6 _____ is someone who wears clothes that are
fashionable.

D Views on fashion

1 Read the article. Then match the two parts of each sentence.

1 Coco Chanel was a woman _____

2 Levi Strauss was the man _____

3 Richard Blackwell was a person _____

a who made the first jeans.

b who wrote about fashion.

c who designed hats and clothing for women.

People Who Changed Fashion

Coco Chanel was a French fashion designer who changed fashion for women. She started making glamorous hats in her apartment. Then a famous actress wore Chanel's hats in a play, and suddenly many women wanted her hats. So Chanel started a business and opened a hat store in 1913. In the early 1900s, women used to wear uncomfortable skirts, but Chanel wanted to be comfortable. She often wore men's pants, jackets, and ties. She started making comfortable and fashionable clothing for women. She made pants and women's suits that were comfortable and trendy, and she began selling them in her store. By 1919, she opened a larger store and was famous in France and other parts of the world. She changed women's clothing, and she inspired other designers.

Levi Strauss had a clothing store in California in the 1870s. His store sold work clothes for men. At that time, working men wore pants that ripped or tore a lot. Strauss worked together with the tailor Jacob Davis to make better pants that were strong and that a man could wear for a long time. They made the pants with a heavy cloth called denim. At that time, there was another heavy cloth called jean. People started to call the denim pants *jeans*. Jeans used to be for work, but they became trendy in the 1950s when teenagers started wearing them. Now many people wear them, even when they aren't working.

Richard Blackwell was an American designer who wrote about fashion. In 1960, he wrote a "Ten Worst-Dressed Women" list in a magazine. People didn't use to talk badly about famous people's clothes, but Blackwell wrote about actresses who wore clothes that he thought were ugly or weird. Today, there are many TV shows with people who give opinions about the clothes that actors and actresses are wearing these days. There are also many websites that have "Worst-Dressed" lists about celebrities.

2 Read the article again. Answer the questions. Write complete sentences.

1 What was the first item of clothing Coco Chanel made?   *She made hats.*

2 Why did Chanel sometimes wear men's clothing?   _____

3 Why did Levi Strauss make pants from denim?   _____

4 Who made jeans trendy?   _____

5 Who did Richard Blackwell write about?   _____

Interesting lives

A Have you ever been on TV?

1 Look at the pictures. Check (✓) the correct sentence for each picture.

1 ✓ I often get seasick.
☐ I often lose my phone.
☐ I often win an award.

2 ☐ I moved to a new city last week.
☐ I was on TV last week.
☐ I acted in a play last week.

3 ☐ I met a famous person in New York.
☐ I broke my arm in New York.
☐ I was on TV in New York.

Excellence in Business

4 ☐ I got seasick at work.
☐ I broke my arm at work.
☐ I won an award at work.

5 ☐ I used to act in plays.
☐ I used to be on TV.
☐ I used to win awards.

6 ☐ We're meeting a famous person.
☐ We're acting in a play.
☐ We're moving to a new city.

2 Complete the chart. Write the past participles. Then write R (regular) or I (irregular).

	Base Form	Past Participle	Regular or Irregular		Base Form	Past Participle	Regular or Irregular
1	lose			9	try		
2	be			10	break		
3	act			11	happen		
4	chat			12	do		
5	see			13	meet		
6	win			14	move		
7	have			15	eat		
8	go			16	get		

3 Complete the conversation with the present perfect forms of the verbs in parentheses. For answers to questions, use short answers.

Joe Hey, Marta. _____Have_____ you ever
   1
_____been_____ (be) on TV?
   1

Marta Yes, I _____have_____ . I was interviewed
   2
about the Japanese language school I went to
in Tokyo. Hey, _____ you ever
   3
_____ (visit) Japan?
   3

Joe No, I _____ .
   4

Marta It's great. I studied there for a month.

Joe What did you like the best?

Marta The food! _____ you ever _____ (try) sushi?
   5   5

Joe Yes, I _____ . I like Japanese food. I also like Korean
   6
food. _____ you ever _____ (try) Korean food?
   7   7

Marta Yes. I _____ . A few times. _____ you ever
   8   9
_____ (go) to South Korea?
   9

Joe No, I _____ . But my sister _____ (be) there. She went to Seoul.
   10   11

Marta I hear they have good food at the markets in Seoul. _____ she ever
   12
_____ (eat) at a night market?
   12

Joe Yes, she _____ . She _____ (have) food at
   13   14
night markets lots of times.

Marta That's cool!

4 Look at the chart. Then write questions and short answers with the words in parentheses. Use the present perfect.

	play table tennis	do karate	break a bone	act in a play	be on TV	chat online
Emily	✓			✓		✓
Ken		✓	✓			✓
Sandra		✓		✓		✓
Marcos		✓		✓	✓	✓
Julia	✓			✓		

What have you done?

1 (Emily / break a bone)

   Question: Has Emily ever broken a bone ? **Answer:** No, she hasn't .

2 (Emily and Ken / be on TV)

   Q: ? A: .

3 (Ken / play table tennis)

   Q: ? A: .

4 (Sandra / do karate)

   Q: ? A: .

5 (Marcos / chat online)

   Q: ? A: .

6 (Marcos and Julia / act in a play)

   Q: ? A: .

5 Look at the chart in Exercise 4. Write sentences about what you have and haven't done. Use *never* for negative sentences.

Example: I've played table tennis lots of times.
            I've never done karate.

1 _____

2 _____

3 _____

4 _____

5 _____

6 _____

B What I mean is . . .

1 Cross out the expression that doesn't belong in each list.

1 Are you saying . . .	Do you mean . . .	What I mean is, . . .
2 Do you mean . . .	What I'm saying is, . . .	I mean . . .
3 What I mean is, . . .	Does that mean . . .	What I'm saying is, . . .
4 What I'm saying is, . . .	Does that mean . . .	Do you mean . . .
5 Does that mean . . .	I mean . . .	Are you saying . . .
6 What I'm saying is, . . .	Are you saying . . .	What I mean is, . . .

2 Circle the correct words to complete the conversation.

Jenny I'm really sleepy.

Amy Really? Why?

Jenny I didn't sleep last night.

Amy (Do you mean) / I mean you didn't get any sleep?
1

Jenny Well, no. **What I mean is,** / **Does that mean** I didn't get *much* sleep.
2

Amy That's too bad. It was better for me. I couldn't stay awake!

Jenny **What I'm saying is,** / **Are you saying** that you slept a lot?
3

Amy Well, yes. **I mean** / **Do you mean** I slept all night . . . for about eight hours.
4

Jenny Oh. What time do you usually go to bed?

Amy I go to bed about 10:00 p.m., and I never use an alarm clock in the morning.

Jenny **What I mean is,** / **Does that mean** you get up late in the morning?
5

Amy No. . . . **What I'm saying is,** / **Are you saying** I wake up early. I always wake up
6

at 6:00 a.m. I don't need an alarm.

Jenny That's nice. I never wake up early without an alarm.

an alarm clock

C Life experiences

1 Look at the pictures of Roger and Mary's trip. Then complete the email with the correct expressions from the box.

climbed a mountain	tried an extreme sport	went to a spa
tried an exotic food	✓ went camping	went whale-watching

1

2

3

4

5

6

Hi Lorena and Bill,

We're having a lot of fun in Canada with our friends. Victoria is a beautiful city. Last weekend we

_____*went camping*_____ near the ocean. It was great. We
                   1

_____ on Saturday, and we _____
            2   3

on Sunday. Roger and I even _____ : zip-lining. You go through the
                                              4

air from tree to tree! It was exciting!

This week, we're staying in a nice hotel. We had dinner at a very nice restaurant in the hotel last

night. I _____ . I ate broiled rainbow trout with fiddleheads and rice.
                        5

Rainbow trout is a delicious fish. Fiddleheads are an exotic vegetable. I even

_____ at the hotel with Barbara. Can you believe it? It was very
             6

relaxing. Roger and Tim didn't go.

I have to say good-bye now. We're going to an amusement park in Vancouver, a big city near

Victoria. I can't wait to ride the roller coasters!

Write soon,

Mary

2 Complete the sentences with the correct forms of the words in parentheses.
Use the present perfect or the simple past.

1 I _'ve been_____ (be) to Mexico lots of times.

2 My sister _____ (eat) at a Turkish restaurant yesterday.

3 Paulina _____ (never / go) to a spa, but I _____ (go)
   to one last month.

4 _____ you ever _____ (try) an extreme sport?

5 I _____ (try) skiing last year, but I _____ (not / like) it.

6 _____ Jorge and Vanessa _____ (ride) a roller coaster at
   the park yesterday?

7 What countries _____ you _____ (be) to in the past?

8 My cousins _____ (go) camping last week, but I
   _____ (never / go) camping before.

3 Write questions to complete the conversations. Use the present perfect and the simple past.

A. **Hyun-ju** Hey, Matt. _Have you ever gone camping_____?
                                              1

   Matt   No, I haven't. But my sister went camping last weekend.

   Hyun-ju Really? _____?
                                     2

   Matt   Yes, she did. She had a lot of fun.

   Hyun-ju _____?
                                     3

   Matt   No. She didn't climb a mountain, but she went kayaking.

   Hyun-ju Wow! _____?
                                     4

   Matt   No, I have never gone kayaking. But I'd like to go sometime.

   Hyun-ju Me, too!

B. **Josh**   How was your vacation, Nicky?

   Nicky   It was great! _____?
                                          1

   Josh   No, I didn't get your postcard. _____?
                                                            2

   Nicky   I sent it on Monday. It's from Mexico City.

   Josh   Cool!

   Nicky   _____?
                                3

   Josh   Yes, I have. I went to Mexico City last year.

   Nicky   _____?
                                4

   Josh   Yes, I saw the pyramids. They were amazing!

   Nicky   Great! You're going to like my postcard!

4 Look at the chart. Write sentences about what Victor has done using the information in the chart. Use the present perfect or the simple past.

		never	last year	a few years ago	lots of times
1	swim		✓		
2	play golf			✓	
3	do yoga	✓			
4	join a gym			✓	
5	lift weights				✓
6	climb a mountain	✓			
7	play soccer				✓
8	try karate		✓		

1 _Victor swam last year._   5 _____

2 _He_ _____   6 _____

3 _____   7 _____

4 _____   8 _____

5 Answer the questions with your own information. Write complete sentences. If your answer is no, add more information.

Example: _Yes, I have. I found it on the beach._   *or*

            No, I haven't. I don't take my phone on vacation.

1 Have you ever lost your phone on vacation? If yes, did you find it?

   _____

2 Did you go on vacation last year? If yes, where did you go?

   _____

3 Have you ever tried an extreme sport? If yes, did you like it?

   _____

4 Have you ever won an award? If yes, why did you win it?

   _____

5 Have you ever met a famous person? If yes, who did you meet?

   _____

6 Have you ever gotten seasick? If yes, where were you?

   _____

1 Read the article. Write the correct question from the box before each answer.

| Is it dangerous? | Are *caving* and *spelunking* different? | What is *spelunking*? |

The Life of a Spelunker

We interviewed Karen Osgood, a woman who has been spelunking for over 15 years. Read what she says about this interesting activity.

Q: _____
              1

A: *Spelunking* is another word for *caving*. It's an interesting activity. People go in caves and walk around in them. For example, I walk around and look at the rocks in caves, and I take pictures. I often have to walk through water, and I sometimes see waterfalls in caves. There is a lot of climbing, too.

Q: _____
              2

A: No, not really. Well, what I mean is that some people say *cavers* are serious about the activity and *spelunkers* aren't. They say *spelunkers* go in caves for sport or fun and *cavers* go in caves to explore and learn new things. But many people use the two words in the same way. Of course, scientists who study caves for their job are called speleologists. They know a lot about biology, physics, and chemistry. I'm not a speleologist, but I know a lot about caves. I'm serious about it, too, so I guess I'm a caver. But it's OK if you call me a spelunker!

Q: _____
              3

A: Yes, it is. People need to be very careful. Caves are often wet because of water, and you can fall down. You should also wear safety hats and good boots. You sometimes need to wear warm clothing because caves are usually cold. It's very important to take lights, too. You can't see anything without them. I have a light on my hat, so I don't have to hold one in my hand. Oh, and never go in a cave alone. I always explore caves with two or three other people.

2 Read the article again. Then write T (true) or F (false).

1 Karen has been spelunking for many years.
    _T_

2 People don't climb in caves. _____

3 There's sometimes water in caves. _____

4 Spelunkers study caves as part of their job. _____

5 There isn't a lot of light in caves. _____

6 You should always go caving with other people. _____

Our world

A Older, taller, and more famous

1 Label the things in the picture with the correct words.

1 canal _____
2 b _____
3 tu _____

4 p _____
5 su _____
   sy _____

6 to _____
7 sk _____
8 st _____

2 Put the words in the correct order to make sentences.

1 is / the Akashi-Kaikyo Bridge in Japan / older / The Tower Bridge in England / than / .
   The Tower Bridge in England is older than the Akashi-Kaikyo Bridge in Japan.

2 the Erie Canal in the United States / than / is / The Murray Canal in Canada / shorter / .

   _____

3 more / The Sydney Harbor Bridge in Australia / is / than / modern / the Tower Bridge in England / .

   _____

4 as / long / the Channel Tunnel between England and France / The Lincoln Tunnel between New Jersey and New York City / is / not / as / .

   _____

5 tall / the Sears Tower in the United States / is / The Jin Mao Tower in China / not / as / as / .

   _____

6 the London Underground / people on it / has / The New York City subway system / more / than / .

   _____

7 as / as / large / the Zócalo square in Mexico City / is / The Plaza Mayor in Madrid / not / .

   _____

3 Circle the correct words to complete the paragraphs.

There are many skyscrapers in Hong Kong. Two very tall skyscrapers are the Bank of China Tower and Central Plaza. Central Plaza is **more tall than** / (**taller than**) the Bank of China Tower. It also has **more floors** ₁
than / **more floors** the Bank of China Tower. The Bank ₂
of China Tower is **older than** / **older** Central Plaza. But it looks ₃
more modern / **more modern than** Central Plaza. ₄

I. M. Pei created the Bank of China Tower, and Dennis Lau and Ng Chun Man created Central Plaza. Some people say that I. M. Pei has created **more famous buildings than** / **more than famous buildings** ₅
Dennis Lau and Ng Chun Man. He has made buildings around the world. For example, he made the John F. Kennedy Library in Boston and the pyramid at the Louvre Museum in Paris.

Bank of China Tower   Central Plaza

Hong Kong

4 Read about the bridges. Then write comparisons with the words in parentheses.
Use -er endings or *more . . . than*.

The Brooklyn Bridge, New York City

The Golden Gate Bridge, San Francisco

1 The Brooklyn Bridge is 1,825 meters long. The Golden Gate Bridge is 2,737 meters long. (is / long)

   The Golden Gate Bridge is longer than the Brooklyn Bridge.

2 The Brooklyn Bridge is 26 meters wide. The Golden Gate Bridge is 27 meters wide. (is / wide)

3 The Brooklyn Bridge opened in 1883. The Golden Gate Bridge opened in 1937. (is / old)

4 The cost to build the Brooklyn Bridge was $15.5 million. The Golden Gate Bridge was $35 million. (was / expensive)

5 It took 13 years to build the Brooklyn Bridge. It took four years to build the Golden Gate Bridge. (took / time to build)

6 Each day, 145,000 people go on the Brooklyn Bridge. Each day, 118,000 people go on the Golden Gate Bridge. (has / people on it each day)

5 Change sentences 1–4 from Exercise 4. Use *not as . . . as*.

1 *The Brooklyn Bridge is not as long as the Golden Gate Bridge.*

2

3

4

1 Complete the conversation. Use expressions for expressing disbelief and for saying you don't know. The first letter of each word is given.

Tyler Hey, Susana, look at this.

Susana What is it?

Tyler It's information about the plazas in Mexico. There are more plazas in Mexico than anywhere else in the world!

Susana _I don't believe it!_
        1

Tyler And we're in a very famous plaza – the Zócalo. Do you know another name for it?

Susana I h_____ n_____ i_____.
              2

Tyler It's also called Constitution Plaza.

Susana That's interesting. But I like the name Zócalo better. . . . How old is it?

Tyler I r_____ d_____ k_____. But the plaza is older than some of the buildings
              3
around it.

Susana S_____?
      4

Tyler Yeah. There used to be different buildings around the plaza, but over the years people built new buildings in place of some of the old ones.

Susana N_____ w_____! I wonder why the old ones are gone. . . .
         5

Hey, do you know how big the square is?

Tyler It says here it's 240 meters long and 240 meters wide.

Susana That's pretty big! Hey, I'm hungry. Is there a restaurant near the plaza?

Tyler I d_____ h_____ a c_____! Maybe there are some ideas in this book.
              6

2 Complete the conversations with one of the expressions from Exercise 1. More than one answer is possible.

1 **A** Do you know how long the Channel Tunnel is?

  B _____

2 **A** Wow! Did you know the Danyang-Kunshan Grand Bridge is the longest bridge in the world?

  B _____

C World geography

1 Complete the puzzle with words for geographical features. What's the mystery word?

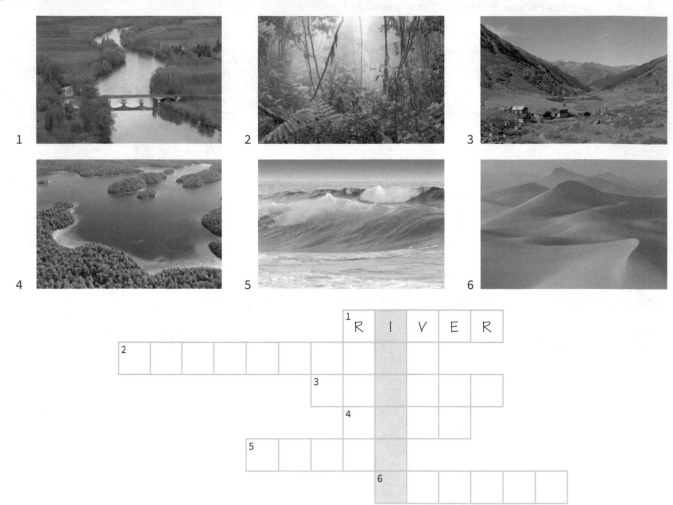

1

2

3

4

5

6


```
                              ¹R  I  V  E  R
        ²☐ ☐ ☐ ☐ ☐ ☐ ☐ ☐
                          ³☐ ☐  I  ☐ ☐
                            ⁴☐  V  ☐ ☐
                  ⁵☐ ☐ ☐  E
                        ⁶☐  R  ☐ ☐ ☐ ☐ ☐
```

2 Complete the sentences with words for geographical features.

1   The Nile _____ *River* _____ is 6,650 kilometers long.

2   A _____ is extremely dry and hot.

3   We swam in a small _____ on vacation.

4   The Indian _____ has less water than the Atlantic or Pacific.

5   Maui is a beautiful _____ surrounded by the Pacific Ocean.

6   I went to the Amazon _____ _____ last winter. The trees and other plants were beautiful, and I saw a lot of animals, but it really rained a lot!

7   When we went camping last summer, we put up our tent in a _____ next to a river. Every morning, we looked up at the mountains all around us. It was great!

8   The most famous _____ in the United States is Niagara Falls.

3 Complete the text with the correct superlative forms of the adjectives in parentheses.

Yosemite National Park

Yosemite National Park is one of ___the most beautiful___ (beautiful)
                                        1
parks in the United States, and it's one of _____
                                                        2
(large) parks in California. There are many interesting geographical
features in Yosemite. Yosemite Valley is _____
                                                    3
(popular) place to visit in the park. It's easy to walk around in the
valley. Tuolumne River is _____ (long) river in the
                                      4
park, and there are many river trips you can take. There are also many
waterfalls to see in the park. Yosemite Falls is _____ (high) waterfall.
                                                              5
Chilnualna Falls is one of _____ (difficult) to see because it's behind rocks.
                                        6

January, February, and March are _____ (wet) months in Yosemite. Spring
                                                7
is _____ (good) season to see waterfalls. Summer is
          8
_____ (hot) season, and it's also the _____ (busy)
          9   10
season. There aren't many visitors in the park in the winter because it's very cold.

4 Look at the chart. Write sentences with superlative nouns.

In the Caribbean			
	Aruba	**Cuba**	**the Dominican Republic**
1 land	180 km^2	110,860 km^2	48,670 km^2
2 people	104,589	11,477,459	9,794,487
3 rain (each year)	21.3 inches	52 inches	54.5 inches
4 official languages	2	1	1
5 TV stations	1	58	25

1   _Cuba has the most land._ _____
2   _____
3   _____
4   _____
5   _____

5 Complete the sentences with the superlative forms of the underlined words.

1 **A** We're going to New Guinea this year. It's an extremely <u>large</u> island.

  B Yes, it is. But Greenland is ___the largest___ island in the world.

Greenland

2 **A** This street has a lot of cars. Is there always this much <u>traffic</u>?

  B Yes, First Avenue gets ___the most traffic___ in the city.

3 **A** My uncle does research in the Antarctic Desert, and he says it's really <u>cold</u>.

  B I know. The Antarctic Desert is _____ desert in the world.

4 **A** What a great day! Let's sit in the <u>sunshine</u>.

  B OK. This is _____ we've had all summer!

5 **A** Wow, this is beautiful! We're up so <u>high</u>. What a great view!

  B Did you know Lake Titicaca is one of _____ lakes in the world?

6 **A** I'm going to Japan. Where is a <u>good</u> place to see temples?

  B I think Kyoto is one of _____ places to see temples in Japan.

7 **A** I'm tired of being <u>wet</u> on this vacation! It has rained every day on this trip.

  B Well, May is usually _____ month in this city.

8 **A** How many <u>people</u> live in New York?

  B Over 8 million. It's the city in the United States with _____ .

6 Answer the questions with your own information. Write complete sentences and use superlatives.

Example: The longest bridge I've ever been on is the Golden Gate Bridge.

1 What's the longest bridge you've ever been on? _____

2 Where's the highest place you've ever been? _____

3 What's the most beautiful place you've ever seen? _____

4 Where's the hottest place you've ever been? _____

5 What's the tallest building in your town? _____

6 What's the longest river in your country? _____

7 Which city in your country has the most people? _____

8 Which month gets the most rain in your town? _____

39

D Natural wonders

1 Read the article. Then write the name of the correct natural wonder under each picture.

1 _____ 2 _____ 3 _____

Canada's Seven Wonders

CBC TV and radio stations had a contest to choose the Seven Wonders of Canada.
People sent their ideas to a website and voted for their favorites.

People's Choices	Votes
Sleeping Giant This is a long peninsula in Lake Superior, which means it has water on three sides. From across the lake, it looks like a big, sleeping person!	177,305
Niagara Falls These amazing waterfalls are on the border of Canada and the United States. There are three waterfalls, but the largest and most beautiful is called Horseshoe Falls, and most of it is in Canada.	81,818
Bay of Fundy This is a large body of water where the Atlantic Ocean meets part of Canada. It has the highest tides in the world. The water from the ocean comes in 17 meters higher than when it goes out!	67,670
Nahanni National Park Reserve This beautiful national park in northern Canada has rivers, waterfalls, mountains, forests, birds, fish, and other animals.	64,920
Northern Lights These are colorful moving lights in the sky. The best time to see them is on very dark, cool nights in March, April, September, and October.	61,417
The Rockies The Canadian Rockies are beautiful, high mountains that have sharp peaks and wide valleys. They are cool and wet, but the tops have no trees because it is too cold and rocky for them to grow.	55,630
Cabot Trail This 950-kilometer hiking trail through part of the Cape Breton Highlands has some of the most beautiful views in Canada. It is named after John Cabot, an Italian man who explored the land in 1497.	44,073

2 Read the article again. Then answer the questions.

1 Who had the contest for the Seven Wonders of Canada?   *CBC TV and radio stations*

2 Which place had the most votes? _____

3 Which ocean's water goes into the Bay of Fundy? _____

4 What are the best months to see the northern lights? _____

5 How long is the Cabot Trail? _____

Organizing your time

A A busy week

1 Complete the phone conversations with words from the box.

✓birthday	business	doctor's	soccer
blind	conference	job	violin

A. **Jake** Hey, Ramon. Can you come to my

_____birthday_____ party on Saturday?
1

Ramon I'm not sure. I have a _____
2

appointment at the hospital at 2:00 p.m. What time is

the party?

Jake It starts at 4:00 p.m. And there's someone

I want you to meet. Her name is Olivia.

Ramon Well, I can come to the party. But I don't know about Olivia. I've never

been on a _____ date.
3

Jake It's not really a date. You're both just going to be at the party. It'll be fun!

B. **Yae-jih** Hi, Don. How are you?

Don OK. I'm a little nervous about my _____ interview at TGL Bank.
1

Yae-jih Oh, right. When is it?

Don Today at 2:00. Mr. Lawrence and Mrs. Nelson have a lot of _____
2

meetings, so we are going to have a _____ call. I won't have an
3

interview face-to-face.

Yae-jih Wow. That's different. Good luck!

C. **Laura** Hello, Sibel. Do you want to have lunch tomorrow?

Sibel I'm sorry. I can't. I have a _____ lesson tomorrow.
1

How about on Saturday?

Laura I have _____ practice in the afternoon.
2

Let's have dinner on Saturday night.

Sibel OK, great. And we can go to a movie after dinner, too.

2 Circle the correct words to complete the email.

Hi Jim,

How are you? Thanks for your email. It will be great to see you next week. What (are you doing)/ do you do on Thursday? I have tickets to a hip-hop concert, if you'd like to go with me. **It's starting** / **It starts** at 8:00 p.m. **I'm having** / **I have** soccer practice at 4:00, but **it's ending** / **it ends** at 5:30. If you can go to the concert, we could meet for dinner at 6:30 at Oh Boy Pizza. What do you think?

Also, are you busy on July 28th? **I'm moving** / **I move** that day. Could you help me move? Katie and Mike **are helping** / **help** me, too. They **are going** / **go** to a yoga class every Saturday from 8:00 to 10:00 a.m., so we'll start at 11:00. **I'm buying** / **I buy** lunch for everyone.

I hope you can go to the concert. Write soon or call me!

Raul

3 Check (✓) the correct sentences. Rewrite the incorrect sentences with the correct forms of the verbs. Use the simple present or the present continuous.

1 ☐ Lorena is having a violin lesson every Thursday.

   Lorena has a violin lesson every Thursday.

2 ☐ Do you have any doctor's appointments next week?

   _____

3 ☐ Marvin picks up his sister in Miami at 3:30 p.m. on Saturday.

   _____

4 ☐ Brenda and Tom are staying at my house this weekend.

   _____

5 ☐ Naoki plans a conference call in meeting room B for Tuesday next week.

   _____

6 ☐ The movie starts at 9:00 and is ending at 11:30.

   _____

4 Read the sentences. Check (✓) if the event is happening right now or in the future.

		Now	Future
1	I can't have lunch now. I'm studying for my biology test.	✓	☐
2	I have a doctor's appointment on Friday.	☐	☐
3	Jen is working late next week.	☐	☐
4	I'm making sandwiches. Do you want one?	☐	☐
5	I'm sorry. Tae Jung isn't here. He has soccer practice.	☐	☐
6	Melanie can't go on a blind date on Saturday. She has a guitar lesson.	☐	☐
7	We're leaving for vacation in three days!	☐	☐
8	Larry isn't answering his cell phone. He is on a conference call.	☐	☐

5 Complete the calendar with your own plans for next week. Write sentences with the present continuous or the simple present.

Example: **Sunday** _I have gymnastics practice._ *or* _I'm visiting my aunt and uncle._

WEEKLY CALENDAR

Sunday	
Monday	
Tuesday	
Wednesday	
Thursday	
Friday	
Saturday	

B Can I take a message?

1 Put the words in the correct order to make sentences for leaving and offering to take phone messages.

1 leave / want / a / message / to / you / Do / ? _Do you want to leave a message?_

2 Amber called / him / Please / tell / that / . _____

3 is at 12:15 / the conference call / her /
Can / you / tell / that / ? _____

4 know / in the morning / that / you / her / Could /
let / we're leaving / ? _____

5 like / to / you / Would / leave / message / a / ? _____

6 take / a / message / I / Can / ? _____

2 Complete the conversations with sentences from Exercise 1. Each sentence in Exercise 1 is used once. Sometimes, the first word is given.

A. **Brandon** Hello?

Amber Hi. Can I speak to Jim?

Brandon I'm sorry. He's not here. Do

    you want to leave a message ?
            1

Amber Sure. _____
                    2

    _____ .

While You Were Out
For: _____ _Jim_ _____ **Date:** _October 2_
Message: _Amber called._ _____
_909-555-1234_ _____
_____
_____

B. **Victoria** Hello?

Marcos Hello. Can I speak to Tonya, please?

Victoria Um, she's busy right now. Can _____ ?
                                                1

Marcos Yes. We have a business meeting at work tomorrow.

    _____ ?
            2

Victoria 12:15. OK. No problem.

C. **Emma** Hello?

Asami Hi. Is Kendra there?

Emma No, she isn't. Would _____ ?
                                        1

Asami Oh, sure. I'm picking her up tomorrow for a camping trip.

    _____ ?
            2

Emma OK. What time?

Asami About 10:00 a.m.

44

C Can you do me a favor?

1 Circle the correct phrase to complete each conversation.

1 **A** Algebra is difficult.

   B Do you want some help?

   A Yes. Can you **help me with my résumé** / **check my homework**?

2 **A** That restaurant is too expensive.

   B I know, but the food is really good. Let's go.

   A Well, OK. Could you **lend me some money** / **water my plants**?

3 **A** Hi, Ed. It's Sherry.

   B Hi, Sherry. You're calling me early. Is there a problem?

   A Yes. My car isn't working. Can you **check my homework** / **give me a ride to work**?

4 **A** Look at those flowers! Your garden is so beautiful!

   B Thanks. Would you mind **watering the plants** / **getting the mail** with me?

5 **A** Julia is so nice. She always wants to help.

   B I know. She's **feeding my cat** / **giving me a ride** while I'm on vacation.

6 **A** Do you want to go to a movie tonight?

   B I'm sorry, I can't. I'm **getting my mail** / **picking up my parents at the airport**.

7 **A** I need to find a job.

   B My office needs some new workers.

   A Really? That's great. Could you **help me with my résumé** / **pick me up**?

8 **A** Does anyone stay at your house when you travel for work?

   B No. My neighbor usually **gets my mail** / **checks my homework**.
      And he also feeds my fish.

2 Complete the conversation with words from the box.

| ✓can you do | I'll clean | I won't forget | would you mind cleaning |
| could you take | I'll cook | Would you make | |

Tina Matt, _____ can you do _____ me a favor?
                              1

Matt Sure, Tina. What is it?

Tina I'm going to be home late tonight, around 7:00.

_____ dinner?
                     2

Matt No problem. _____ tacos
                                    3

and rice and beans.

Tina Oh, that sounds great! And _____
                                               4

out the garbage? It has to go out tonight.

Matt Definitely. _____ . I promise!
                              5

Tina Thanks. Oh, and _____ the apartment? Our new neighbors,
                                    6

Jay and Camille, are coming over for dinner. Remember?

Matt Um, OK. I guess _____ it before I make dinner.
                                    7

Tina Thanks. You're the best!

3 Rewrite the questions. Use *would you mind*. Then complete the responses with *will*.

1 Can you check my homework?

   A _____ Would you mind checking my homework? _____

   B No problem. _____ I'll check _____ it after dinner.

2 Could you pick me up at 10:30 a.m.?

   A _____

   B Not at all. _____ at any time you want me to.

3 Would you give me a ride to my doctor's appointment?

   A _____

   B No problem. _____ you a ride in my new car!

4 Would you tell Josh that the meeting is tomorrow?

   A _____

   B No, I don't mind. _____ him when I see him at lunch.

5 Could you water the plant in my office while I'm out next week?

   A _____

   B No problem. _____ it. How often should I do it?

4 Look at Eric's notes. Then complete his conversation with each person.

give me a ride to the airport	Priya
feed my fish	Chuck
feed my cat	Chuck
get my mail	Amira
pick me up from the airport	Greg

1 **Eric** Can you give me a ride to the airport on Monday afternoon?

  Priya No problem. _I'll give you a ride to the airport._ What time?

2 **Eric** Can _____ while I'm on a trip next week?

  Chuck Sure. _____ them.

  Eric And would you mind _____ , too?

  Chuck No, I don't mind. _____ it, too.

3 **Eric** Would _____ when I'm on my trip?

  Amira All right. _____ it on Wednesday and Friday.

4 **Eric** Could _____ at 4:30 on Sunday?

  Greg Yeah, sure. _____ and _____ be late!

5 People are asking you favors. Write their questions and your own answers.

1 **Ed** _Can you take our picture_ ?

  You _____ .

2 **Mai** _____ ?

  You _____ .

3 **Chris** _____ ?

  You _____ .

4 **Mara** _____ ?

  You _____ .

47

Perspectives on time

1 Read the article. What are four ways that people waste time?

1 _the Internet_   2 _____   3 _____   4 _____

A Waste of Time!

Many people don't manage their time well. They often find other things to do when they should be working. Some people don't even know they are wasting time. These are some of the top time-wasters. Do any of them sound like you?

1 The Internet is a very useful tool, but it's also the biggest way people waste time. Many people play games or chat online instead of working or doing research for school. Have you ever looked at a funny video instead of working?

2 TV can be interesting and educational, but many people waste time by watching TV. Have you ever taken a short break from work to watch "just a little TV" and then hours later thought, "Oh, that's right. . . . I was doing laundry."?

3 People can actually waste a lot of time when they text. At work, some people text too much about personal things instead of doing their jobs. Other people have the same problem at home. They text with friends instead of doing chores.

4 Believe it or not, thinking can be a waste of time. Some people think about work, but they don't do it. They even make to-do lists, but then they just think about all the things they have to do, and they never get them done!

2 Read the article again and the sentences below. Did each person waste time?
Check (✓) Yes or No.

	Yes	No
1 Vicky researched information on the Internet for a work report.	☐	✓
2 Dan played a game online for two hours at work.	☐	☐
3 Ines watched TV for ten minutes and then finished her homework.	☐	☐
4 Haluk texted his boss about a business meeting.	☐	☐
5 Sam texted his co-worker about his son's soccer game.	☐	☐
6 Jen made a to-do list, and then she thought about how she'd never finish all of it.	☐	☐